A Common Sense Approach to Sustainability

Accelerating profitability through aligning your people and processes with the environment

Tammy A.S. Kohl
Resource Associates Corporation

Contributing Authors: Betsy Allen, Jim Godshall, Jerry Hogan, Susan Lauer, Rick Lochner, Jean Oursler, Adam Pressman, Robyn Rickenbach and Susan Bacher, Arnold Rintzler, Greg Stuart, and Grant Tate

A Common Sense Approach to Sustainability

Contents

Contents

/

Sustainability as a Mega Trend: Is it Right for Your Organization?

- INTRODUCTION -

The world around us is ever changing. The opportunities and challenges of business are always evolving. Throughout recent decades business has been exposed to mega trends that have positively contributed to permanent change in the way business thinks, leads, and operates.

What is a mega trend? It is a large, over-arching direction that shapes the business world for a decade or more. There have been many mega trends that have impacted business such as the quality movement, laptop computing, and social media. Now a new mega trend is emerging in the area of the environment. It is called sustainability.

The mega trend of sustainability is built on the foundation of protecting our planet and its resources. It has become part of a global commitment to protect the environment while providing a future for many generations to come. While sustainability was introduced over two decades ago, it is still far from cresting. The true application of sustainability is much broader and runs much deeper, especially for businesses. Society is demanding organizations become responsible corporate citizens and many consumers are putting their money behind those decisions. They are buying the products of, advocating for, and supporting organizations committed to sustainability.

Business sustainability emerged out of the concept of being or going green. Due to outside pressure from community special interest groups and in an effort to meet new regulatory requirements, some industries have been forced to change how their processes and products impact the environment and their customers. While they may have been reluctant at first, what early adopters came to realize is the powerful impact of business sustainability on the environment and their bottom line. Early adopters have seen a tremendous benefit in the areas of profitability, customer satisfaction, stakeholder benefits, and community relations due specifically to their business sustainability initiatives.

Although many early adopters are large companies like Walmart, Proctor & Gamble, Philips, 3M, Adidas, The Coca-Cola Company, GE, Boeing, Cisco, IBM, Nike, and McDonalds to name a few, organizations of all sizes can implement business sustainability and reap the benefits of this mega trend. The question is, how?

The purpose of this book is to help you with the how. This book will provide a common sense approach to incorporate sustainability throughout your organization in order to protect and conserve resources while positively impacting your bottom line.

No organization should tackle sustainability without first understanding its strategic intent. An organization needs to understand what it is doing, why it is doing it, and what it is going to measure. Most importantly, sustainability requires commitment from the senior leadership team of the organization. "You cannot implement these kinds of programs bottom up; it is impossible. It is always top-down, always. Because it is a cultural change, you cannot do it organically." Georges Kern, CEO, IWC (International Watch Co.) Therefore, if you want to grow your business through sustainability then it has to be driven by senior leadership. It is not a program that is implemented, but a business strategy that is defined and aligned through your people, processes, and the structure of your organization.

According to Walmart's President and CEO, Mike Duke, "The fact is sustainability at Walmart is not a stand alone issue that is separate from or unrelated to our business. It is not an abstract or philanthropic program. We don't even see it as corporate social responsibility. Sustainability is built into our business. It is completely aligned with our model, our mission, and our culture.

Simply put, sustainability is built into our business because it is so good for our business.

Sustainability helps us deliver on our Every Day Low Price business model. Using more renewable energy, reducing waste, and selling sustainable products helps us take costs out of the system. This year, for instance, we surpassed our goal of achieving 25% greater fleet efficiency. The savings from this and other sustainability initiatives translate into lower costs and lower prices for our customers."

So why have small and midsize businesses found it difficult to embrace sustainability as a business practice? Most organizations not forced to comply with regulations need to be presented with measurable reasons, a return on investment, as to why embracing or incorporating a new strategy like sustainability makes sense. Early adopters like Walmart, IBM, Nike, and GE are measuring value in key business areas and smaller organizations can too. It is our experience that the outcomes large companies have achieved are just as possible in the small and midsize markets. Examples of those benefits include:

- A stronger brand

- Improved customer loyalty

- New revenue sources

- Access to new markets

- Stronger pricing power

- Process and operational improvements – efficiency/effectiveness

- Lower costs

- Greater ability to attract employees

- Increased employee productivity and loyalty

- More efficient use of resources

- Innovation

The benefits are real. Take a look at a smaller organization that has embraced a sustainability strategy and is seeing a return on its investment of time and resources.

Case Study

Johnson Financial Group—founded in 1970, it is a full service financial services company that employs 1,267 people. As a privately held company, the leadership team believed showing its customers Johnson's commitment to keep operating costs down in tough economic times was a message of strength. Johnson's sustainability campaign focuses on improving operations while generating social, environmental, and economic success. Its current campaign includes:

- Reducing transportation

- Development of green buildings

- Reducing energy use

- Education

- Paper reduction and recycling

- Waste reduction

The results are clear. Johnson Financial has reduced energy consumption at its corporate headquarters for three consecutive years. One project alone saved 500,000 kilowatt hours of electricity, 17,000 therms of natural gas, and eliminated more than one million pounds of carbon dioxide per year.

What does this mean in terms of dollars? Use a sample rate of 15¢ per kilowatt x 500,000 kilowatt hours of electricity, and it generates a savings of $75,000.00. In our experience most small to midsized organizations can use an extra $75,000.00.

....

The process of embracing sustainability is similar no matter what industry you are in or the size of your organization. After senior leadership has made the commitment, sustainability needs to be specifically defined for your organization. If the definition is not specific to your organization it will not be successful. Once defined, the next step is to build a sustainability framework and incorporate that framework into your overall strategic plan. You must align your structure to support sustainability, align your people's knowledge and attitudes to implement it, and put metrics in place to measure results.

At this point, you may put this book down and say it is not worth it, but it is only a matter of time until sustainability is no longer a new strategy but rather a permanent thread in the fabric of society and a requirement for all successful businesses creating the next wave of progress.

According to the SBA, small firms represent 99.7% of all U.S. employee firms; they employ over one-half of the private sector, and they have generated 64% of the new jobs over the past fifteen years. It is clear that small and midsize organizations are a significant economic driver for the U.S. economy and will not be exempt from the driving forces of sustainability. Ignoring sustainability is bad for business, no matter the size of your organization.

If your organization recognizes that sustainability is not going away and positions itself as a sustainable organization, you can achieve a sizeable competitive advantage. Those organizations that capitalize on business sustainability will benefit not just by optimizing resources but increasing their bottom line as well.

Jeffrey Immelt, CEO of General Electric is quoted as saying, "As CEO, my job is to get out in front of it (sustainability) because if you are not out in front of it, you're going to get plowed under."

Is your company going to be in the forefront of business sustainability or get plowed under? The choice is yours.

Defining Sustainability: What is it?

- CHAPTER ONE -

When you decide to incorporate sustainability into your business practices, the first step to starting your sustainability efforts is to define what sustainability means for your organization. Developing your own definition is critical in order to get buy-in for your sustainability strategy. Unfortunately, many senior leaders who decide that they should include sustainability as a business practice often look at it as tactical, not strategic. Additionally, many only see it as an environmental issue and not as an organization-wide strategy.

The term sustainability appeared in the 1987 report by United Nation's World Commission on Environment and Development (The Brundtland Commission) entitled *Our Common Future*. The Brundtland report simply defined sustainability as follows: *to meet the needs of the present without compromising the ability of future generations to meet their own needs.*

Despite this definition, many organizations continue to either misunderstand sustainability or just do not know how to define what it is for their organization. Others can define it but do not know how to implement it. Misunderstanding sustainability is evidenced in many studies and is exemplified in a survey published by Boston Consulting Group and MIT. Their survey revealed that there is no single established definition for sustainability. The study also clearly states, although companies differ in their definition, sustainability is a force to be reckoned with and a concept that is here to stay.

The size of your organization does not matter. If you do not define what sustainability means to your organization, you will not be able to implement or measure it successfully. Many organizations that initially engaged in sustainability defined it only in terms of the environment. As sustainability becomes a normal course of business, organizations are beginning to include economic, customer, stakeholder, and governmental areas in their sustainability definition.

The question for senior leadership within any organization is: What does sustainability really mean to our business? Frequently, senior leadership teams lack not only a definition but also a full understanding of how to incorporate or apply the concepts of sustainability to their strategic plan, their operating processes, their employees, their customers, and stakeholders. When implemented properly, sustainability can have a measurable and positive impact on the environment, generated by the organization's people and processes resulting in improved profitability. Organizations that have defined what sustainability means to their businesses and who have a focused implementation model are seeing significant benefits. Based on the documented success of early adopters, sustainability has provided a sound business case of creating value through innovation and employee involvement.

Take a look at how three very different organizations define their sustainability initiative and review some of the great results they are currently achieving. These examples will reinforce the point that sustainability is a very individualized initiative.

Case Studies

Patagonia, an outdoor apparel and gear company and a leader in sustainability defines sustainability as: *Build the best product, cause no unnecessary harm, use business to inspire and implement solutions to the environmental crisis.*

Due to its sustainability strategy, Patagonia has created an interactive web site, *The Footprint Chronicles,* where consumers can literally track the environmental impact of products from design through delivery. For the sake of this example we selected and tracked their Rain Shadow jacket. The Rain Shadow jacket is designed in Ventura, California; the fabric is purchased from Nagoya, Japan; the jacket is sewn in Hanoi, Vietnam, and the completed jacket lands in Reno, Nevada for distribution. Here is the environmental impact for one Rain Shadow jacket.

- Energy consumption in production/shipping: 40 kilowatts equal to burning an 18 watt compact fluorescent light bulb for 93 days (24 hours a day)

- Carbon produced: 32 pounds equal to 47 times the weight of the jacket

- Waste generated: 5 ounces equal to slightly one-half the weight of the jacket

- Water consumed from origin through garment delivery: 213 liters equal to drinking water for 71 people for one day

Another leader in sustainability is **SAP AG**, a German software corporation. They define sustainability as: *We strive to create a better run world where organizations balance short and long term profitability, holistically manage economic, environment, and social risks and opportunities.* As model 1.1 at the right illustrates, their results are real.

Model 1.1

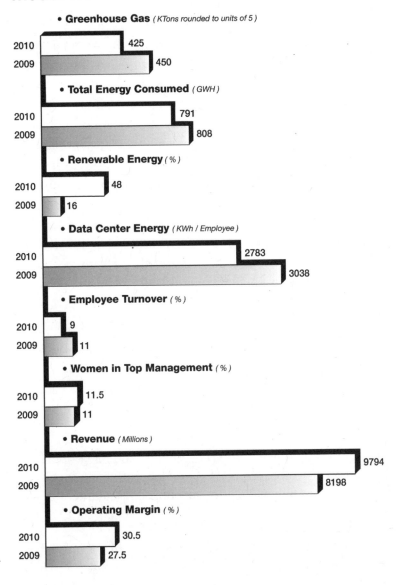

Berea College is located in Berea, Kentucky—founded in 1855, and employs 485 people.

Berea is one of seven work colleges in the national Work College Consortium. The college focuses on providing a strong academic program as well as a holistic approach to social and environmental issues. Berea is unique in that it charges no tuition and admits only academically promising students primarily from the Appalachia area who have limited resources. Every student works 10-15 hours per week in more than 100 college offices, departments, and programs off campus while carrying a full academic schedule. The eighth and current President, Dr. Larry Shinn, strongly believes "sustainability is one of the very best tools low-income students can use to succeed, whether they return to a small Appalachian town or, like some of our graduates, go on to Wall Street. Our philosophical framework is built around educating ourselves and our students on sustainable living."

Some of their initiatives include:

- Renovated historical buildings and residence halls using sustainable features and were retrofitted often using recycled materials

- 1,200 of their 8,200 acres of land and forest are used to grow local foods and provide instruction in the agriculture and natural resource curriculum

- Developed the first ecological village in Kentucky designed to consume less than 75% of energy and water compared to conventional housing

- Built a central plant to Leadership in Energy and Environmental Design (LEED) standards which reduced the ecological footprint of the college by reducing energy consumption and is a major factor in their goal of 45% less energy usage by 2015

Due to these initiatives and the college's long-term commitment to sustainability, Berea College used 52% less BTU's (British Thermal Unit) of natural gas in 2009 over its 1999 usages and provides 15% of its cafeteria food from its own farm and local producers.

....

So, how will your organization define sustainability? One working definition that many of our clients use is:

> **Sustainability is an increase in productivity and/or reduction in consumed resources without compromising product or service quality, competitiveness, or profitability while helping to save the environment.**

From a business model perspective this definition speaks to the environment while focusing on improving measurable business results. Specific definitions of sustainability will continue to remain somewhat unique based on industry, products, services, regulations, etc. However, the underlying foundation of the Brundtland definition remains: *to meet the needs of the present without compromising the ability of future generations to meet their own needs.*

Taking the time to define what sustainability means to an organization, its customers and stakeholders, and to know how its products and services impact the environment is the first and most important step for two reasons. The first reason is it allows an organization to focus on a common objective. The second reason is it provides buy-in to the impending changes that must take place.

One of the best places to start is to review your vision, mission, and values. These three statements, as part of your strategic plan, can help you focus on what you want to achieve with your sustainability initiatives. Additionally, you may want to ask your employees what sustainability means to them. Ask them how they would define it and how they would describe the organization's future in this area. Empowering employees and getting their buy-in early on, not only will help define your sustainability initiatives but because of their early involvement, you will be implementing sustainability initiatives and seeing results more quickly.

As you develop your sustainability definition, remember to keep your message simple, personal, and doable. Sustainability can't be viewed as a program du jour. It is a strategic choice that requires senior leadership's commitment and the alignment of all processes and people within the organization.

After sustainability has been defined, the next step is to implement a framework that will support the definition and pay it off with environmental as well as financial results. If sustainability is going to become an embedded value in an organization's culture this step will become never-ending.

For many small and midsize businesses, there has been no pressing need to build a strategy for sustainability. Many early adopters of sustainability were forced to implement a strategy due to customer and stakeholder demands or regulations. In our experience, successful implementation is enhanced when an organization begins by understanding its strategic intent. It is not difficult but an organization needs to understand what it is doing, why it is doing it, and what it is going to measure.

Answering the following questions can help a senior leadership team create a clear focus and direction.

- What definition of sustainability is best for your organization to adopt?

- What desired results does your organization want to accomplish and in what time frame?

- How will you measure those desired outcomes?

- How will you communicate your sustainability plan and establish buy-in with your employees and stakeholders?

These questions are important and need to be addressed before any implementation begins. And, of course, the answers to these questions need to be blended with your existing strategic plan. If your organization does not have a strategic plan, it will be critical to develop one that includes sustainability.

Questions to Ask Yourself:

1. What is your organization's definition of sustainability?

2. Was your adoption based on regulation, pressure from customers or stakeholders, or internally driven?

3. Who is or should be accountable for sustainability in your organization?

Sustainability:
A Competitive
Advantage or Pitfall?

- CHAPTER TWO -

Unless forced by regulation, many small to midsized organizations may only consider the adoption of a sustainability strategy based on documented financial value. Often senior leadership considers the principle objective of the organization to be profitability, and they look at new or stricter environmental regulations and/or higher demands from customers and stakeholders about sustainable products and services as profitability inhibitors. Business history has proven that change always provides new opportunities. Ironically organizations of all sizes have been closed minded or slow to accept change and new ways of thinking.

Defining what new opportunities an organization can generate from a strategy of sustainability is definitely a trade up not a trade off.

It has been documented in many studies that an integrated strategy of sustainability will lead to measurable results and financial benefit.

Depending on your organization the opportunities for enhanced business can be dramatic. A study conducted by Boston College Center for Corporate Citizenship and the Hitachi Foundation (published in 2010) verified several business opportunities generated by sustainability initiatives. It provides a comprehensive view of small, medium, and large businesses in the United States. (See Model 2.1)

Every outcome listed on the next page has a direct and positive impact on an organization's bottom line. When implemented properly, sustainability creates both a financial and a competitive advantage.

The facts are clear; sustainability through environmental excellence is here to stay. It will remain a mega trend for an extended period of time as it morphs into the fabric of what businesses do every day. It just makes common sense. Your organization and industry may not be charged with regulations, but it would be naïve to believe that future regulation is not possible.

Model 2.1

(The State of Corporate Citizenship in the United States 2009, a study conducted by Boston College Center for Corporate Citizenship and the Hitachi Foundation surveyed 756 executives. 36% of the sample represented small companies (1-99 employees), 24% represented medium companies (100-999 employees), and 40% represented large companies (1,000+ employees).

If your industry is lucky enough to remain unregulated, it is almost guaranteed your customers and stakeholders will require you to change your business practices. Our research indicates that in most cases companies will be faced with both regulations and customer and stakeholder pressure. William Mulligan, Environmental Affairs Manager at Chevron Corporation, makes a comment that reflects our experience. "Over the last decade, we have seen many polls confirming the importance of the environment to Americans. Only an irresponsible company would dismiss this trend as a passing fad or fail to recognize the need to integrate environmental considerations into every aspect of its business. Environmental excellence has to become part of strategic thinking. It is in our best economic interest to do so. In fact, whenever we are forced to change, we often find opportunities for growth and improvement."

In many markets, embracing sustainability is fast becoming the price to compete. It is similar to the quality movement in the eighties. Although many industries and companies fought the concept of quality, remember how everything changed when a clear financial case could be made for the implementation of quality initiatives. Quality quickly became expected and was accepted by business based on its ability to improve profits. As quality became expected, customers started to demand high quality and speed. Organizational push back was not quite as strong, but as soon as companies saw they could generate additional profits based on the combination of quality and speed, they looked for ways to take time and variation out of business processes to serve customers better and faster. Sustainability comes to the business environment in a similar fashion. If an organization is not forced to create sustainable products and services through regulation or customer and stakeholder pressure, it will be not accepted unless there is a solid business case with a clear return on investment.

However, where and how does an organization start? For a business to become truly sustainable, a change is needed. Failure to do so can result in a reactive situation where an organization suddenly finds itself unable to compete. Integrating a strategy of sustainability may seem daunting. It can look and feel like a huge commitment of human resources, money, and time which is often translated into expense without a return on investment. Organizations can tackle this just like the answer to the age-old question, how do you eat an elephant? The answer—one bite a time. So too, it is with any major initiative like sustainability. Integrating a strategy of sustainability begins by assessing where you are relative to stakeholder expectations combined with your definition of sustainability, then taking one step at a time to close the gap. Not unlike many large business objectives, they can only come to fruition because they are broken down into smaller and more manageable action steps. The process we have used successfully to help organizations embark on a sustainability strategy is documented in Model 2.2 pictured on page 16. The key question that needs to be answered at Level One is, why does an organization want to proceed?

Model 2.2

A Common Sense Approach to Sustainability

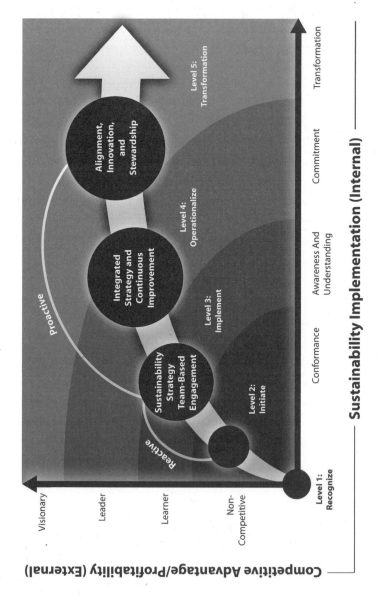

Level One

In our experience, organizations within Level One as defined by their own actions, can be categorized in one of two groups:

- Group One – 'have to'

- Group Two – 'it is not necessary'

'Have to' organizations are implementing sustainable initiatives because they are forced by customers, stakeholders, or regulations to conform to certain standards and guidelines. In this case, they are reacting and viewing the process as compliance. Therefore, it is seen as an expense not an investment. They see no business benefit ... only forced requirements. This is sometimes referred to as the "thou shall" business strategy. It is a requirement that is forced upon the organization as a commandment from outside forces.

The 'it is not necessary' group is not getting forced by outside agencies to comply, so they do not see a need for a formalized sustainability plan. They take a minimized approach. This group also sees little to no business benefit to move forward with sustainability. Therefore, senior leadership is not focused on environmental processes and social issues.

We find the most important driver to help an organization move from Level One to Level Two is education—not just education on the concepts and the power of sustainability, but also education on how sustainability can be a powerful business driver and provide financial gain.

Level Two

Level Two is still a level of non-competitive conformance but because organizations at this level are often being forced to comply, there is a forced sense of knowledge and awareness. It is hard to successfully follow the rules if you do not know what the rules are. Organizations at this level are typically doing what is necessary to comply and will typically look for quick wins that may generate a positive business impact. This level is still a reactive level so there are few, if any, communicated objectives, and the employees have not been asked to engage in the concepts. It is all about compliance and quick wins.

Level Three

At Level Three we see a huge shift as senior leadership openly adopts sustainability as a strategy and they clearly see the ability to achieve positive business outcomes. Senior leadership has created a sustainability vision and has identified and communicated clear objectives organization-wide. Due to the clear communication and emotionalized vision, employees are becoming engaged and can more clearly see their contribution to the success of the strategy. Larger sustainability projects are identified with defined metrics. In general, the entire organization is committed to learning how sustainability applies to it and its stakeholders.

Level Four

In Level Four, we see serious traction as the sustainability strategy is embraced by the entire organization. It is leadership driven and interdepartmental teams are collaborating cross-functionally. The organization is in a proactive mode with organization-wide commitment to continuous improvement and sustainability. There is a clear understanding of the relationships between environmental impact, cost, and risk. It is becoming how the organization does business and it is starting to become a defining aspect of its culture. The strategy is becoming integrated into the fabric of the organization. From a planning perspective, detailed action plans for the next two to three years have been created.

Level Five

Implementing a strategy of sustainability is never-ending. At Level Five we see a total integration of the strategy to the point where it is now part of the organization's culture. It is ingrained throughout the entire organization within all processes and employees' actions to the point where they no longer have to think about their actions—they are just doing the right thing. There is a visionary transformation of sustainability and stewardship with standards other organizations look to as a benchmark of excellence.

As an example, Dell was named Newsweek's 2010 Greenest Company in America. Dell communicated in their 2011 Corporate Sustainability Report that while they are proud of their sustainability record, the transformation process is never-ending. Trisa Thompson, Vice President of Corporate Responsibility for Dell reinforces that corporate belief in a recent quote, "Whether it is through our green efforts or giving programs, our company gives back in many ways responsibly and with integrity. While we have made much progress, we have much more work to do to help people achieve their full potential and help us protect the planet."

Organizations who focus on aligning their processes, people, and structure while creating a culture of sustainability are generating some of the best results an organization can accomplish and perhaps have ever seen!

Questions to Ask Yourself:

1. If your customers/stakeholders rated your organization on its sustainability initiatives, how would the organization fare?

2. Are you currently a 'have to' or an 'it is not necessary' organization?

3. In your organization, what are the top three desired results that could be positively impacted by implementing a strategy of sustainability?

4. What are your customers'/stakeholders' greatest concerns regarding sustainability?

5. How do those concerns relate to your products or services?

The Role of Leadership: Who is Really in Charge?

- CHAPTER THREE -

How would you define the difference between leadership and management?

Our experience is leaders focus on the future, innovation, and where the organization is headed, i.e. determining what the right things are for the organization to do. In contrast, management's role is to do the right things right and do them now.

Both roles are necessary and both roles are important, one without the other will produce great plans but no results. While the other will produce the frustration of being ready but having no place to go.

One fact we consistently observe in our clients is for any organizational change to be successful it requires commitment from senior leadership. New strategies and initiatives require change. Positive change requires senior leadership to provide a clear vision of where this change will take the organization and how a strategy of sustainability would benefit the organization, the employees, and their stakeholders. Commitment and ongoing follow-up by the senior leadership team is also critical. No new strategy can survive, let alone thrive, if senior leadership is not fully on board.

To help organizations who are in the early stages of Level One (Recognize) or Level Two (Initiate) get started, here are a few important questions for senior leadership to consider.

- What does sustainability mean to your organization?

- Does sustainability make sense for your organization at this time?

- How does sustainability align with your current strategy and other initiatives?

- What is your organization's specific business case for pursuing sustainability?

Another way for senior leadership to determine where they are and where they want to go in the area of sustainability is to conduct a readiness assessment. Providing your employees and management with the opportunity to share their thoughts on where the organization stands on its sustainability issues anonymously is invaluable and informative. An assessment provides a data driven starting point that will give the senior leadership team the necessary information to better answer the questions listed previously. You may also learn that your organization is doing more than you think as it relates to recycling, waste reduction, etc. which should be recognized. If the data and the business case support the decision to move forward with a sustainability strategy then the education, communication, and planning process begins.

> **Feel free to experience a sustainability mini assessment at http://theinstituteforsustainability.com**

This next series of steps is senior leadership's most important job. After the assessment has been completed and the baseline created, sustainability is rolled into the organization's strategy. A sustainability definition, a framework, a vision, and clear objectives are created and communicated organization-wide, employee engagement is encouraged, and stakeholder research begins.

Large organizations (Walmart, Nike, GE) are beginning to align their business' mission with sustainability, but what if you are not a large company? All the better! Smaller organizations are far less encumbered. Senior leadership within smaller and midsized organizations often have a greater ability to recognize opportunity and capitalize on it quickly. They can often set up systems allowing greater employee engagement; they are more nimble at making decisions, and there is almost always less bureaucracy. Results can happen quickly and speed speaks volumes. Quick wins are what provide positive traction for any initiative and they get people excited about wanting to do more. Here are some case studies that reflect our experience.

Case Studies

A small manufacturing company increased its capacity within one week by participating in a tailored cycle time reduction process saving 1.2 million dollars. This company redesigned its production scheduling and work-in-process to better utilize its existing resources. Creating less waste and better utilization of existing resources is part of this organization's definition of sustainability.

A family owned business reduced the amount of time it took to produce approved kitchen designs by 56% while reducing scrap by 34% after participating in a custom designed sustainability process. Creating less scrap is better for the environment as well as more profitable for the company. Customers continue to win by receiving an on-time, quality product at a competitive price; the environment wins by having less waste being sent to a landfill, and the business wins by having less expense per unit produced.

A community hospital (270 beds) was looking for ways to improve its overall effectiveness in the community and to its patients. The hospital elected to embark on a three-year improvement plan that started with the development of a strategy and was followed by the implementation of a management development process designed to improve the skills and attitudes of the management team. Core processes were revised and waste was eliminated. This resulted in improved financial performance, improved patient, physician, and employee satisfaction, decreased average length of a patient stay, and improved environmental impact by decreasing waste and costs.

A medium sized manufacturing company reduced rework, scrap, and waste in the production of pre-stressed concrete beams by creating a more efficient process of producing and communicating changes in specification drawings between sales, engineering, and production. In one week, the implemented solutions generated millions of dollars in annualized savings. Because the employees were involved in creating the new process, their loyalty to the company increased resulting in fewer grievances, more satisfied customers, less landfill requirements, and increased conservation of water and energy.

Ensuring business sustainability through increased profits, revenues, and loyal customers is a natural outgrowth of adding a strategy of sustainability to your existing strategic plan. It is for these reasons senior leadership of every organization needs to seriously address the value of sustainability to their business. A recent sustainability award recipient at the 2011 Ceres Conference[1]. Anvil Knitwear (a small private business apparel manufacturer) was asked why they took on sustainability as a priority. Caterina Conti, Anvil's CAO responded, "I don't think you can afford not to. We have saved million and million of dollars. It is just dollars you leave on the table."

1: Ceres is a nonprofit organization that leads a national coalition of investors, environmental organizations, and other public interest groups working with companies to address sustainability challenges such as global climate change and water scarcity.

In fact there are some very strong opinions from early adopters who believe that organizations that do not embrace sustainability will create a business deterrent. This is clearly echoed by John Replogle, former President and CEO of Burt's Bees, "Sustainability is no longer optional. Companies that fail to adopt such practices will perish. They will not only lose cost basis; they will also suffer in recruiting employees as well as attracting customers."

During Nike's acceptance speech at the Ceres Conference, Hanna Jones, Vice President of Sustainable Business and Innovation stressed: "Sustainability is no longer a values based question. It is a core strategic imperative for any company that intends to thrive and grow in the years ahead."

Anvil, Burt's Bees, and Nike all began with a vision of sustainability. After a sustainability vision is in place, objectives have been identified, employees have been asked to be engaged, and senior leadership remains committed to drive and support the initiative, it is time to get into the nitty gritty of implementing the action steps.

Now, it is all about making it happen!

Questions to Ask Yourself:

1. Is senior leadership committed to a strategy of sustainability?

2. How would your organization benefit if you were to adopt a strategy of sustainability?

3. What is stopping you from implementing a sustainability strategy?

4. If you implemented a strategy of sustainability, how would stakeholder opinions change?

5. What are some quick wins you can implement?

Level Three: Implement Knowledge, Power, Structure, and Measurement

- CHAPTER FOUR -

Quick wins are a great way to give your sustainability strategy momentum and demonstrate to everyone sustainability does indeed provide value to the organization, your community, and the environment. Level Three is all about taking it to the next level. That means creating awareness and understanding at all levels within your organization to drive your sustainability strategy through team-based engagement. As Dale Carnegie is famous for saying:

> **"Knowledge isn't power until it is applied."**

Effective and consistent communication is key to success in Level Three. Of course, no strategy achieves success without significant employee buy-in and engagement. Often, employees can be skeptical about new initiatives. They may suspect the new program is just a lot of hype or the next program du jour. A carefully crafted communication strategy is vital to your sustainability process. It is critical to make sure the communication process includes detailed information as to why the company is headed in this direction, who is leading the charge, what projects are under way or about to get under way, and how those projects progress.

To demonstrate the priorities and potential outcomes of projects consider using a Project Value Chart. This chart will clearly and quickly prioritize, communicate, and demonstrate the payback of each project against the estimated time required to implement the project.

Model 4.1

Project Value Chart

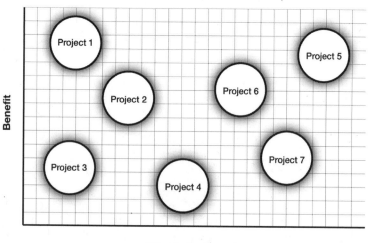

To fully understand how to use this chart begin with the two axes. The vertical axis represents benefits which can be measured by tangible or intangible outcomes. The higher up a project falls on the vertical axis the greater the benefit or outcome. The horizontal axis represents the time needed to implement. Projects that fall further to the left happen more quickly than projects that fall further to the right of the horizontal axis. As an example, if a project has a high benefit and is relatively quick to implement it would appear in the Project 1 location. On the other hand, if the project is benefit rich but takes a relatively long time to implement that project might appear in the Project 5 position.

Depending upon the time increments, those projects to the left of center might be considered relatively short-term projects, while those to the right of center are more long-term projects. As senior leadership decides how to allocate resources, both short term and long term projects should be considered. Unless there are high priority strategic or stakeholder concerns it may be beneficial to go after the projects that produce higher benefits more quickly.

As an exercise, if senior leadership in your organization identified the following sustainability projects, where would you place the projects on a Value Chart like Model 4.1?

1. Reduce landfill waste by 5%.

2. Reduce water usage by 50%.

3. Reduce the time it takes to change over a machine by 20% to provide greater efficiencies and better customer response time.

4. Eliminate scrap in the manufacturing process by 80%.

5. Answer customer phone calls within three rings to provide faster response time.

6. Implement a recycling program.

7. Conduct an energy audit.

8. Conduct an organizational assessment to determine the organization's readiness to implement a sustainability strategy.

Model 4.2

Project Value Chart

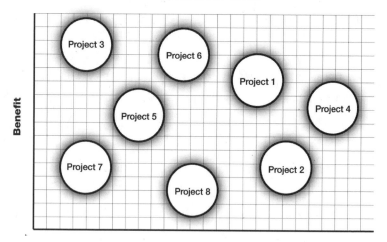

Time to Implement

Given these options, projects 3, 5, and 6 would be relatively quick to implement and would have relatively high values. Projects 7 and 8 would be quick and perhaps even necessary but will provide a lower value. Projects 1, 2, and 4 probably have a medium to high value but are longer in term. (See model 4.2)

Depending on your business, you may need more parameters to measure progress and payback. Strategize with your management team or the cross-functional teams directly connected to the project to specifically define the desired outcomes for each sustainability project. These defined outcomes should include both tangible and intangible benefits such as increased revenue (tangible) and increased employee loyalty (intangible).

Computer data is an important tool but visible graphics can create instant focus and are a good way of keeping score. This type of chart is a great dashboard to guide senior leadership's decisions, and it is a great communication tool for management and employees. Consider posting a project value chart in a conference room or in a place where all employees can see it. Use the organization's intranet to provide fast progress reports as projects move forward.

Another model that can be a great communication tool and is equally as visual is the balanced scorecard model (See Model 4.3 on page 34). In theory and practice, the balanced scorecard can be used as a management tool to bring to life a strategic plan by aligning business activities with the vision and strategy of an organization. Breaking the strategic plan into four interacting components and then defining the objectives, measurements, targets, and initiatives for each of the four, puts detailed actions behind a strategic plan. The four balanced categories are financial, customer, internal business processes, and learning and growth.

Model 4.3

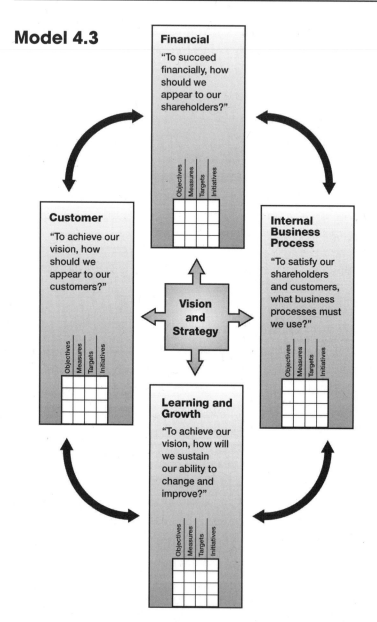

Adapted from Robert S. Kaplan and David P. Norton, "Using the Balanced Score Card as a Strategic Management System," Harvard Business Review (January-February 1996): 76.

Originators, Drs. Robert Kaplan and David Norton of the Harvard Business School, contend this model adds a non-financial performance measurement framework to augment traditional financial metrics. This framework provides senior leadership with a more balanced view of an organization's performance. In their experience senior leadership teams need such a system because they are over reliant on finances. While important, financials are not necessarily good predictors of future strength but rather indicators of past decisions.

We believe sustainability now becomes the fifth area of measurement. The following describes each of the five areas in more detail.

Learning and Growth refers to employee training and corporate attitudes relative to individual and corporate growth. However, learning is more than just training; it also includes access to coaches, individual development plans, and mentors as well as the ease of communications among employees including technology.

Business Process refers to internal business and operating processes. The metrics should indicate how well the business is running and how well products and services are conforming to customers' requirements. This category, when improved using cross-functional teams, can produce exceptional results quickly by taking out waste, excessive non-value added time, and variation.

Customer focuses on the importance of satisfying or exceeding the expectations of the purchasers/users of your products and services. When done thoughtfully and consistently they will become loyal to your organization. The size of your loyal customer base is a leading indicator of your future success and market strength. The more loyal customers you have the better.

Financial perspective refers to the traditional financial data collected and analyzed by an organization. The balanced view indicates that while this is important data it should be viewed in relationship to the other categories. This balanced perspective allows senior leadership to measure and predict future strength.

Sustainability refers to your ability to meet or exceed the expectations of your stakeholders relative to their environmental concerns and your actions. The stakeholder category is larger than just your customers. A stakeholder is anyone who is impacted by your organization's activities and can include the community, your supply chain, customers, shareholders, etc.

For organizations that are currently using the balanced scorecard model and are adding sustainability as a strategic initiative (Model 4.4 at the right provides an example) it may make sense to add a box to the original four, labeled **Sustainability** (how do you want to appear to your stakeholders as stewards of the environment). Your sustainability strategy would then be broken down into its own objectives, measurements, targets, and initiatives.

Model 4.4

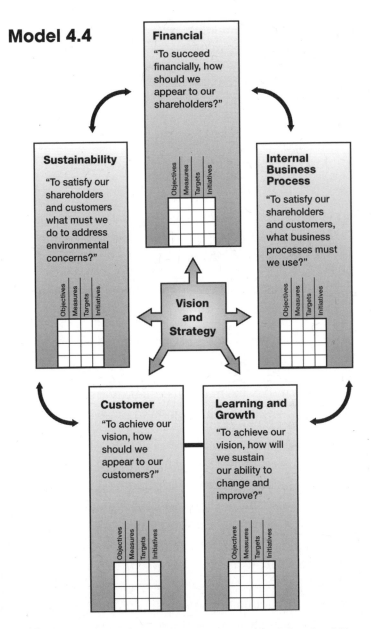

Adapted from Robert S. Kaplan and David P. Norton, "Using the Balanced Score Card as a Strategic Management System," Harvard Business Review (January-February 1996): 76.

Here is an example of adding your sustainability initiative into the balanced scorecard model:

- **Strategy:** Become concerned stewards of the environment.

- **Objective:** Eliminate all landfill waste.

- **Measurements:** Amount of waste taken to the landfill.

- **Target:** By the end of this fiscal year, we will no longer need to contract with our waste hauler to take any waste to the landfill.

- **Initiatives:** Assemble a cross-functional team to identify the source of our landfill materials.

  » Work with our supply chain to reduce waste coming into our location.

  » Identify what materials can be reused or recycled and implement a program of reuse and recycle.

It will become management's responsibility to emphasize the current projects by reviewing them in staff meetings and by carefully tracking and reporting progress and success. Creating and distributing a periodic sustainability report is also an effective way to highlight the importance of sustainability to the organization's success. It has been proven that success breeds success, so use your communication process as a way to spark new interest and new ideas. All communication should remind readers that sustainability is not just about going green.

> **In reality, your organization's sustainability initiative aims to reach the much higher goal of business sustainability, which means positioning the organization to be successful both short and long term, providing employees with long-term opportunities, and an environmentally sound and rewarding place to work.**

Your communication process should also address external communications to your customers, stakeholders, and the community. Your sustainability strategy should become an integral part of the organization's overall brand, supporting your public image, enhancing credibility, and building corporate responsibility, while at the same time boosting demand for your products and services. In addition to the established sustainability teams, you might consider adding a team to be responsible for all internal and external communications for consistency and timeliness.

Consider using modern communication tools and multiple media outlets including blogs, social media, and other online tools. Social media cuts across both internal and external audiences. These powerful tools can accelerate your information flow and can quickly reach a large audience. Take a proactive initiative with electronic media rather than leaving it to chance. If you don't have a communication strategy and take charge, others can discuss your sustainability processes in ways you cannot control.

Too often we achieve results and then move on to the next initiative never really celebrating the milestones we achieved. Hosting a sustainability celebration can really set you apart in the minds of your employees, your customers, and your community. Consider sponsoring an annual event to let everyone know what you have achieved. Create a sustainability award earned by employees based on success criteria appropriate to your organization's initiatives. Publicly recognize your supply chain for its mutual contribution to enhancing processes while focusing on the environment. Give gold stars to your customers to let them know you appreciate their contributions. By finding ways to celebrate your results, you will increase the awareness of your sustainability program and your efforts which will result in benefits for your organization.

As your sustainability efforts gather momentum your employee engagement will increase. Employees will begin to have and add ideas for saving resources and improving operations. Your sustainability process should include a place where employees can share their ideas, and you may also consider providing rewards, recognition, or compensation for the best ideas. A poorly designed and executed sustainability process will discourage employees, so it is important for your process to be well thought out. Of course, a formal suggestion process is not the only way to collect and recognize employee creativity. Managers and team leaders should encourage their team members to seek and share new ideas and look to implement new ideas directly within the work of the team.

When attacking larger projects the teams will need to consist of members from interdepartmental and multifunctional areas. Organizational structures vary across different organizations, but, in general, teams representing the different elements of the project will have the best chance of a successful implementation. Each sustainability project should be assigned an appropriate team representing all interdepartmental needs. The team will then develop a team charter which is a detailed plan with defined measurements. The detail of the charter should include the project's description, goals, potential benefits, role of each team member, and a time line.

Many of the sustainability efforts will require changes in processes or procedures. In those cases, team members and other employees will need training in process improvement and new process creation techniques. The team charter should include these approved training steps giving the team the full authority to implement the sustainability project.

After a cross-functional or interdepartmental team has been created and they have a charter to follow, the team will also need to engage with the supply chain and those parties who both supply the team and those who get supplied by the team to ensure success. Efforts by the team cannot be nullified or attenuated elsewhere in the supply chain. This can be challenging in organizations and here lies another important role of senior leadership. Senior leadership needs to engage their senior leadership counterparts in organizations along the supply and value chains.

What can't be measured can't be managed. Organizations need to clearly understand the measures of their sustainability efforts. Qualitative measures can begin with the recognition of the voluntary acts bubbling up in the organization and are every bit as important as quantitative measures. Peter Drucker is famous for saying both quantitative and qualitative measures need to be interwoven and are necessary to illuminate change.

The word sustainability not only applies to the organization, but also to the sustainability effort. The implementation of prioritized projects is a step toward making sustainability a way of life in your organization and an integral element of your organization's culture. Sustainability is not a fad. By definition, it is an ongoing component of organizational thinking and documented success.

Questions to Ask Yourself:

1. How are you communicating and engaging your employees in the sustainability initiative?

2. What sustainability measurements are key to your organization?

3. How do you recognize/reward employees who are engaged in the change process?

4. How do you currently use cross-functional teams to tap into the creativity and innovation of those who are closest to your customers and stakeholders?

5. Do you have a process for reporting your sustainability successes?

6. What processes have you realigned in order to support your sustainability efforts?

Level Four: Operationalize— Leaving the Station

- CHAPTER FIVE -

According to Dictionary.com's 21st Century Lexicon, operationalizing means: *to define a concept or variable so it can be measured or expressed quantitatively; to put into operation, start working.*

Operationalizing sustainability within the organization means the culture has embraced the notion of sustainability as a measured part of the day-to-day operations; sustainability is becoming a way of life. The organization has created a vision and a framework enabling the teams to work across departmental boundaries while engaging the supply chain. The organization is on its way to creating a sustainable culture.

At Level Four, sustainability becomes an integral part of an organization's operation and culture and many larger projects are underway. Now, senior leadership will need to decide how sustainability becomes a permanent consideration in every aspect of the business to the point where every decision considers ways to save costs, preserve the environment and resources, and how to use the organization's human energies in the most effective and efficient ways. The language of sustainability has become a part of every conversation. Sustainability is now an element of the supply chain and vendor selection as well as all negotiations. Customers and stakeholders are reaping benefits from an organization whose products and services are produced with optimal use of physical and human resources. Reporting demonstrates results in reduced environmental impact, cost, and reduced business risk as well as increased profitability. Here is a case study of an organization that is clearly by our definition operating at Level Four.

....

Case Study

Standing Stone Brewing Company in Ashland, Oregon

Standing Stone Brewing Company has been recognized as one of the top 100 green businesses in Oregon. They have integrated a practice focusing on protecting and restoring the environment, and supporting the health and happiness of their community, visitors, and employees. As part of their sustainability implementation they offered to purchase bikes for their employees who agreed to bike to work at least 45 times each year. Now this may seem like a fairly simple step; however, it was done as part of an integrated process and has some wide ranging effects on their employees, their processes, the environment, their brand, and their profits.

Here is how it worked:

The brewery received a Business Energy Tax Credit from the State of Oregon to assist in the purchase of the bikes. This covered 35% of the cost of the bikes, and it reduced the cost of the bikes to under $300.00. As part of the same credit process, the State of Oregon also covered one-third of the cost of the large bike rack which provides parking for employees and customers.

Here's how the initiative benefited the company:

Alex Amartico, owner of Standing Stone cites health benefits and improved employee engagement. As many as one-third of the employees who took the offer are on track to exceed the agreed upon 45 days commuting via pedal power. Now 75% of the employees are participating, and they offer free bikes to all who work at Standing Stone for at least 1,000 hours and agree to the 45 trips per year. The brewery has achieved additional visibility and branding by prominently displaying its logo on the bikes. This proved particularly valuable in introducing the brand to tourists. There is increased availability for parking in the congested downtown area making it easier for those customers who want to drive.

This is just one piece of Standing Stone's overall ongoing sustainability commitment. Standing Stone believes in smart resource use.

We Believe

Reduce how we impact our community and planet

Reuse what's left over and avoid single-use products

Recycle by diverting recyclables from the waste stream

Return resources and support to the community

Developed by Standing Stone Brewing Company

By Level Four, early projects have been completed and wins celebrated. Everyone internally and externally is cheering the organization's sustainability initiatives. Within Level Two and Three, employee training and development is introduced whereas at Level Four, sustainability is now fully integrated into all employee training and development processes. Managers are providing ongoing coaching in sustainability and process improvement skills.

Senior leadership can now look at the sustainability objectives and clearly see they are making major progress because many of the high value, quick implementation projects have been completed. As we discussed in Chapter 3, many organizations began their initiative with an organization-wide sustainability assessment. That assessment establishes a base against which to measure the organization's overall progress. A repeat of the assessment during this operationalization stage can provide a comprehensive way to measure overall progress as well as provide an internal benchmark for future decisions and projects.

This assessment process provides a vehicle to continuously engage management and employees in an effort to measure and celebrate the organization's progress as well as help uncover new areas of opportunity or new areas of concern. The assessment process gives senior leadership a chance to say, "We value our people. We want to take a look at where we are, define our successes, identify new areas of concern or gaps, and give our managers and employees a chance to share their thoughts on our progress and/or current issues."

At Level Four it is again time to review the organization's sustainability vision. At this stage, it is valuable to begin building a long-term sustainability vision that will communicate the next phases of the organization's sustainability strategy. It should address what the organization has accomplished and where they are going from here.

A vision is about becoming not maintaining. James Collins and Jerry Porras, authors of *Built to Last: Successful Habits of Visionary Companies,* describe successful companies as being led by executives who empowered all members of their organization to pursue a cluster of objectives of which making money is only one, and not necessarily the most important one. Other objectives include making bold commitments to big, hairy, audacious goals, and focusing on continuous improvement. Think first of what it means for your organization to be a sustainable company. What will be the result of a long-range sustainability plan for your organization, your operations, your employees, and your customers/stakeholders? The answers to these questions can help create the foundation for a compelling long-term vision. Other characteristics of a compelling vision include:

- Clarify the purpose for change

- Describe intent

- Drive cultural change

- Spur a positive image of the future

- Keep it straightforward

Here are some real world examples:

....

Case Studies

Telcom Company

Recognizing the critical link between a healthy environment and sustainable economic growth, we are committed to leading the telecommunications industry in protecting and enhancing the environment. Such stewardship is indispensable in our continued business success. Therefore, wherever we do business, we will take the initiative in developing innovative solutions to those environmental issues that affect our business.

Community College

Ongoing operations result in a minimal negative impact on our natural environment. We are actively engaged in creating ways to positively impact our environment. Continuous learning takes place about our impact on the environment as a college and as individuals. Sustainability is a way of thinking about everything we do. Every staff member takes a personal responsibility for creating and using sustainable practices and principals in our daily work. We integrate sustainability into our relationships and the social fabric of the college.

Furniture Manufacturer

We will be a sustainable corporation. We engage our employees in more sustainable practices, we initiate and use processes that are neutral or improve our environment, and we utilize our resources in ways that create adaptable and sustainable workplace solutions for our customers. We do all of this globally to protect and restore our environment, create economic value and support, and strengthen our community.

....

These examples are meant to stimulate ways senior leadership can come together to design a common vision to lead and sustain the organization over a long period of time. The process of generating a long-term sustainability vision is an important opportunity for senior leadership to turn their best intentions into a viable and inspirational picture of the organization's future state. The vision will then need to have supporting goals and a customized framework to support it as well as an organization-wide plan to integrate sustainability.

Operationalizing sustainability requires time. Visions have multi-year horizons. Strategies, while shorter in practice, require a level of discipline and accountability over several business cycles to embed sustainability into a culture. How long will it reasonably take to change the conversation from, "Why are we doing this?" to "What are we going to do next?" It will depend; every organization's time frame is unique. However, when people throughout the organization are routinely asking the latter question as a matter of course, the organization is well on its way to a sustainable culture.

At Level Four, there is also transparency as the sustainability vision and efforts are communicated consistently to the stakeholders and the community. One of the added benefits of your work is your customers are noticing and are providing feedback. They approve of what you are doing and want to become involved. They are loyal to you and recommend you to their friends and family. They talk about you and your organization not only as one that delivers a quality product or service, but one that does so with sustainable practices.

At this level of sustainability, the organization is committed to initiatives in all three areas: people development, process improvement, and protecting the environment. The exponential benefit of maximizing the efficiency and effectiveness of its employees, its processes, and the environment is paying dividends in innovation, new products, and increased revenue.

Included in its sustainability efforts, Standing Stone Brewing Company saves by feeding its vegetable waste to its chickens and recycling its used vegetable oil through a manufacturer of biofuels, and sends spent hops to local farms. This organization maximizes the talents of its employees by asking them to share in formalized ways.

In their report, *"Unleashed: How New Consumers Will Revolutionize Brands and Scale Sustainability"* (March 2011), BBMG, a brand innovation studio, found that new consumers are consistently looking to make purchases based on alignment with their values and that do not detract from their day-to-day constraints of money and time. Even during the recent recession, 25% of consumers are willing to pay more for sustainable products. The same 25% are also the early adopters who are two times as likely to adopt sustainable services or products, and let fellow consumers know, both the good and bad. Consumers will buy from you because of the breadth of your efforts and the transparency with which you implement sustainability and drive the economy going forward.

At the completion of this stage, the organization has evolved to a new state; a state where sustainability is an inherent part of planning and execution in all elements of the company. Sustainability is a way of life, woven into the culture of the organization, a basic assumption of strong leadership and good management. Level Four is the stage where senior leadership can say without doubt, "We are a sustainable company ... and we can prove it."

Questions to Ask Yourself:

1. What is the long-term sustainability vision for the organization?

2. How is sustainability incorporated into the long-term strategy for the organization?

3. Are current projects aligned with the sustainability vision?

4. How engaged are your employees? How do you know?

5. Are your customers loyal to your product or service? How do you know?

6. How are you measuring your organization's commitment to sustainability?

7. How are you reporting and publicizing your sustainability outcomes?

Level Five: Transformation— What does it look like?

- CHAPTER SIX -

"One of the best kept secrets in America is that people are aching to make a commitment, if they only had the freedom and environment in which to do so." John Naisbitt, author of *Megatrends*

Transformation is difficult to define. We believe transformation is the process of changing by applying a new set of rules. In this case, it is adding the new rules of sustainability to your organization's strategy. Transformation is not defined by incremental change, but rather it is a bold move to become something new, different, and better. Creating transformation through sustainability requires a cultural change and an emotional connection that runs both deep and wide throughout your organization. "A corporation is a living organism; it has to continue to shed its skin. Methods have to change. Focus has to change. Values have to change. The sum total of those changes is transformation." Andrew Grove, Founder of Intel Corporation.

Transformed organizations have visionary leadership who, along with all their employees, vigorously look for areas to interweave their sustainability vision and values. This applies to each employee individually as well as the organization as a whole. These organizations have moved beyond picking the low hanging fruit and being proactive to becoming visionary and innovative. Transformed organizations understand that the risks associated with not implementing sustainability do not just affect their company but also their customers, their stakeholders, and their community as a whole. In fact, there is growing evidence that not integrating sustainable principles presents a greater risk than actually implementing them. The paradigm has shifted. Sustainability transformed organizations are leaders in their field and they set the standards for others to follow. These organizations are clear about their values and purpose. They are public advocates for sustainability and are clearly recognized as outstanding contributors to their community.

Because of the organization's implementation work at Level Three and Four, the organization has made significant progress. The clearly defined long-term vision and objectives have been communicated while goals and action steps have been handed off and are consistently being achieved. When barriers arise, employees work in cross-functional teams to overcome them, and continuous improvement is the prevailing attitude. Employees are also consistently looking for ways to improve themselves through personal development and looking for ways to innovate. This innovation goes beyond their work and ties to the organization's suppliers and community. Sustainable thinking is part of the culture, and it is part of the employees' way of being.

Sustainability reports are made available to the public in multiple formats, and information about sustainability efforts is promoted in an ongoing manner. While a potential benefit, public revelation of their efforts is not purely about self-promotion, but it encourages other organizations to follow, learn from their insights, and participate in sustainability efforts. The organization pulses with a passion for sustainability. These pulses move out into the community and supply chain like the ripples from a rock skimmed across a calm lake—predictably and consistently.

True transformation is as subtle as it is courageous. Transformation can be difficult even with the best strategy, training, and people. Despite a clear and explicit strategy of what sustainability means it can still be a challenge to implement the transformational change necessary to achieve the highest level of sustainability for your organization. Actually, a transformative organization never reaches the highest level because it will purposely raise the bar and ask, "What can be done next?"

When an organization is functioning at Level Five, very exciting things start to happen. Great ideas come forward through the energy of the cross-functional teams and the organization's supply chain. The organization will collectively fuel the "what can be done next," conversation since sustainability is not a one-time meeting but a way of thinking. Organizational sustainability is not one person's job but rather made up of everyone's commitment. Issues, when identified, are solved in a sustainable way. This means solutions include efficiencies considering people, process, and the environment in a holistic way.

Teams solve problems on the spot. They are empowered and they are confident management will back them up. They understand all the components of sustainability so there is no need to remind them of goals, values, or efficiencies. That is how a transformative cultures lives.

The organization is proud and public about its efforts. Communication on sustainability efforts is comfortably rolled into branding, publicity, the organization's web site, blogs, and other marketing and communication formats. The cross-functional team in charge of the communication process delivers the messages clearly and presents them in a timely fashion.

Customers and stakeholders clearly identify your organization as the best. This is true whether you are a product or service oriented company. It is clear to customers and stakeholders and they promote your organization, your product or service, and how important it is to them. Plus your organization is growing financially.

The organization's values are abundantly clear in everything that is done. When something strays from those values, it is simply recognized, corrected, and new processes are implemented. Once an organization achieves transformation it is critical to create ongoing action steps in order to continuously improve. Some of those steps include:

- **Devote** a senior position or depending on the size of the organization a part of someone's job description to focus on sustainability. This person should report directly to the President/CEO.

- **Commit** to clear, attainable, and big, hairy, audacious goals related to future plans and the ongoing development of your employees.

- **Focus** on processes specifically related to the continuous improvement of your employees.

- **Consistently** question the way processes will improve efficiency and align them with the organization's sustainability goals.

- **Monitor** and continue to measure your impact on the environment. Create a long-range view and seek to lead your industry.

- **Work** with your partners, vendors, and suppliers to create innovative solutions that benefit everyone as well as the community. Become a public advocate for sustainability practices.

- **Continue** to monitor measures that relate to sustainability both short and long term.

Transformed organizations are sustainable organizations; they create focus and the intention to stay that way.

Questions to Ask Yourself:

1. What level of sustainability has your organization obtained? How do you know?

2. What are your next steps?

3. What would it mean for your organization if you were to transform the culture to embed sustainability?

4. Do your customers view your organization as a sustainable one? How do you know?

The Results are Real!

- CHAPTER SEVEN -

What would happen if you were able to differentiate yourself from your competition, be the employer of choice, and strengthen ties with your community? These three things can be used as points of differentiation for any size organization. It is sometimes challenging to achieve these three things simultaneously. Yet, the results from your sustainability strategy can help you achieve greater success in these three areas, and it will translate to increased profitability and business sustainability.

Organizations are frequently surprised by the quick results and the immediate impact they achieve from their sustainability processes. There is a great deal of confirming evidence that sustainability initiatives result in benefits that outweigh the costs. According to Darcy

Hitchcock and Marsha Willard in their book, *The Business Guide to Sustainability: Practical Strategies and Tools for Organizations,*

> **"Organizations that focus on the concepts of eco-efficiency (sustainability) increase their market valuation as well as financial performance."**

Most organizations measure their sustainability results in short-term and long-term value. While sustainability results can be measured in the reduction of carbon footprint and landfill waste, etc., results can also be measured in terms of:

- Company reputation

- Customer value

- Employee retention

- Community relations

Short-term results can often be seen in cost savings, efficiencies, and corporate citizenship. Long-term benefits often mean organizations can better anticipate change, continue to be the leader in an industry, and remain sustainable as an organization. Customer and employee retention as well as better community relations are often seen as a result of a successfully implemented sustainability program.

Like any strategy, implementing sustainability into your organization is no different from anything else you do to help your company be more successful. You need to set your short-term and long-term goals, plan implementation, and then measure the results.

Many companies already have sustainability efforts in place that are producing results and do not even realize it. Often times these efforts are labeled with more traditional business terms like customer service, innovation, or employee engagement. They veil what could be considered strides toward sustainability. Uncovering these hidden results can differentiate you from your competition today!

The banking industry provides a great example of hidden opportunities—opportunities they could capitalize on sooner as opposed to later. Online banking allows you to access your bank account from the Internet. Some banks even let you deposit your checks by taking pictures of them with your cell phone. Looking at it through the lens of the customer, online banking offers convenience and banking at anytime and anywhere.

Now take a look at online banking through a lens of sustainability. Because you do not need to drive to the bank to deposit your checks, ask questions about your account, or transfer money, the bank is helping you to reduce your carbon footprint as well as make your life more productive—two elements of sustainability. Online banking makes banking more efficient because it reduces the need for fuel; it eliminates waste like emissions, and it also reduces the effort it takes to bank. Once identified, these hidden results can provide a measurable difference without a great deal of effort on the part of an organization. Here is a case study of an unaware banking organization not maximizing its hidden opportunities.

....

Case Study

A seven branch, community bank is identified as one of the fastest growing banks in its area. Its philosophy is to always have an innovative edge to ensure customer satisfaction. The bank does not believe in brick and mortar but in being able to provide technology allowing customers to complete their banking needs from their home or office.

One of the bank's cutting edge products is called *remote deposit capture.* This product allows customers to deposit checks right from their desk. It is a perfect product for businesses because it eliminates the daily bank run. The daily bank run is just as it sounds. Somebody from the organization takes the deposits, leaves the office, drives to the bank, makes the deposits, and drives back. The daily bank run can cost a company $20,000.00 a year in lost productivity not to mention the costs associated with the actual run as well as the carbon footprint.

Many of this bank's customers talk about the amount of money they have saved by using the *remote deposit capture* product. However, no one talks about the product in terms of sustainability, including the bank. Now put on your sustainability glasses. Imagine what results the bank could communicate from a sustainability point of view in terms of environment, people, process, and profit. Yet the bank's senior leadership continues to miss the sustainability aspects of their own product.

....

Sustainability is a point of differentiation you can use for your business especially in a crowded industry like banking. Make sure your organization looks for all the results from your sustainability strategy, short-term and long-term as well as hidden opportunities.

Achieving results is one thing—letting everyone know what you achieved is another. As previously mentioned, sustainability is a point of differentiation. So how do you use that difference to your competitive advantage? Large companies like Ben and Jerry's, Stony Hill Yogurts, and Newman's Own all speak about their sustainability efforts as a way to connect with their customers. The field is wide open for small and midsize companies to own sustainability space. Sometimes it is hard to be the first, but when you are more profitable because more customers are choosing your organization due to your sustainability efforts, it makes all the difference in the world.

To become a transformative organization in the area of sustainability it is also important to continually get and give feedback. Why? For most companies getting a result is achievement enough. They implement a process, see results, throw a celebratory high five, and go on to the next project. Creating a culture of sustainability is an on-going process if done right. In order to keep positive traction, it is important to ask for feedback from your employees, your customers, your stakeholders, your supply chain, and your community. Through all of that input you can identify if there are bigger or better results that can be achieved. Creating a consistent feedback loop will help guarantee your organization stays in Level Five.

By actively managing your feedback efforts, you will strengthen your sustainability strategy. When to ask is up to you, although quarterly or bi-annually will usually provide enough feedback to ensure your ongoing efforts are achieving maximum results. Maximizing the contribution and innovation of your people by minimizing the environmental impact of waste produced, the use of natural resources, and the complexity of your processes, allows your organization to see an improvement in your financial bottom line. Take a look at what is happening to a company who started embracing a sustainability transformation in the mid-eighties.

....

Case Study

Canadian Tire Corporation is an $8 billion retail operation with over 1,200 stores, over 57,000 people, and four distinct brands throughout Canada. Since the mid-eighties Canadian Tire has been committed to social responsibility with a top-down strategy of progressive practices that guides its work in the areas of ethical business conduct, human rights and employment practices, environmental protection, safeguarding the health and safety of employees, and investing in local communities. During this time Canadian Tire has relentlessly pursued pioneering business practices that grow the business without increasing the net carbon footprint of the company such as eliminating unnecessary packaging while sending zero waste to landfills, and providing innovative products and services that meet customers' needs without compromising future generations.

Since 1999, Canadian Tire has realized an average net of 8.2% annual earnings per share and paid an average annual dividend of 7.7% to its shareholders despite challenging economic times. In an on going, independent, third party survey, Canadian Tire is regularly listed as one of Canada's most highly regarded companies by both consumers and investors.

Canadian Tire's business sustainability strategy goes beyond a green initiative, said Tyler Elm, Vice President of Business Sustainability for Canadian Tire Corporation. "Our goal is to implement sustainable practices that positively impact energy and climate, waste and packaging, and product and service innovation. The end result is a strategy that advances the business while benefiting customers and the environment."

Canadian Tire has proven over a long period of time that there is financial growth to be had through sustainability strategies. This organization has recognized the wisdom of a sustainability vision and action plan.

Sustainability strategies will vary among companies, industries, locations, and demographics but as we have been talking about through the entire book there are universal benefits for any company in any industry. The results are real and they are quite measurable.

Questions to Ask Yourself:

1. How can a strategy of sustainability differentiate you from your competition?

2. Where are your hidden sustainability opportunities, and how can you capitalize on them today?

3. What process is your organization currently using for giving and receiving sustainability feedback?

4. How can sustainability impact your organization's reputation, customer value, employee retention, and community relations?

Making Sustainability Your Own

- CHAPTER EIGHT -

As we have been discussing, sustainability will mean something different to every organization, but the evidence is clear. Adopting a strategy of sustainability just makes good business sense. Our sustainability model was designed based on over thirty years of experience in helping small and large organizations align their strategies, their people, and their processes to maximize desired business results. Adding a strategy of sustainability just completes the model. (Please reference the Sustainability Implementation Model 8.1 on page 68.) Perhaps one of the best ways to bring the model to life is to share its use through the lens of a customer.

Model 8.1

Sustainability Implementation Model

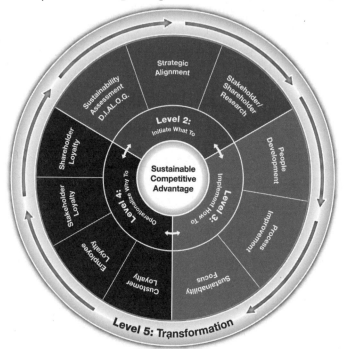

Level 2: Initiate What To
Sustainability Assessment D.I.AL.O.G.
Strategic Alignment
Shareholder/Stakeholder Research

Level 3: Implement How To
People Development
Process Improvement
Sustainability Focus

Level 4: Operationalize Why To
Customer Loyalty
Employee Loyalty
Stakeholder Loyalty
Shareholder Loyalty

Level 5: Transformation

Imagine being asked to join an effort to create a strategic plan, the first ever, for the county in which you live, pay taxes, and vote for county officials. The first two questions after accepting the opportunity to work with the county were where to start and who is really the customer? Similar to a hospital system, there are many customers such as the referring and on-staff surgeons, executives, employees, vendors, patients, etc. The county was no less complicated.

Customer input for a strategic planning process (Strategic Alignment – Level 2) is the wind behind the sails just as the vision is the destination and values serve as the rudder correcting the course. The organization needed, at minimum, to gather feedback from three perspectives: an organizational diagnostic to poll county employees, a citizen survey to poll constituents, and input from the five county commissioners to whom the county manager reports.

The most insightful of the three perspectives was the employee organizational diagnostic tool (Sustainability Assessment D.I.AL.O.G. – Level 2) which we created based on the Malcolm Baldridge Quality Criteria which gathers perspectives about: Leadership, Strategic Planning, Customer and Market Focus, Measurement, Human Resources, Process, Business Results, and Sustainability.

The assessment asks employees throughout the organization to rate leadership's ability to engage them in the vision, mission, and day-to-day decisions. Yet, the most telling question of all was when the assessment asked whether the employees would recommend the county as a place to work. Depending on the department, between 29-50% of the employees, as of the fall of 2009, would not recommend the county to family and friends.

These results led the new county manager to initiate an Executive Leadership development process (People Development – Level 3). The leaders of the 29 departments had little, if any leadership, team building, and goal setting training and development. The manager told us, "When I took over as interim county manager, I had no intention of accepting the permanent role. When it was offered, I deliberated and decided to do so for multiple reasons. First and foremost in my mind was that since I had been the department leaders' peer previously, I knew for the most part, the county's leadership was sound. I also knew that being who I am that I would run the County very differently than the previous manager. Even though I might not like the news, I knew understanding the employees' current perceptions on leadership was critical and it created a baseline for making decisions. Since transparent accountability and collaboration was my vision, I also knew that the top leadership needed to break down any potential silos and really get to know each other on a different level. The executive leadership process helped us make fast progress toward being an accountable, transparent, and community-centered county."

As a result of the process of becoming "transparent, accountable, and community-centered," the county formed the Office of Sustainability and a Citizen Committee for Sustainable Efforts (Sustainability Focus – Level 3). Top of the priority list was increasing the county's social responsibility which has come to be known as sustainability and the first area of focus was the Facilities Services Division.

Up to this point, the facilities division responded to crises and things that were broken. The new facilities manager instituted training for all his people which they did not have access to prior and put a process in place to make preventative maintenance standard. With preventative maintenance, there were fewer crises. The cost of maintaining facilities went from $4.72 per square foot per year to $2.52 while facilities doubled. The facilities manager is quoted as saying, "I am not an environmentalist or even crazy about sustainability. Yet, when I see a viable sustainability idea, it seems to always make good business sense."

Several key members of the facilities department led their first continuous improvement process (Process Improvement – Level 3) to reduce energy usage because their cost of energy per square foot was simply too high as compared to other facilities organizations. The county was one of the initial members of United States Green Building Council LEED (Leadership Environmental Efficiency of Design).

From the beginning they realized that only with the support from people who occupy a building could true reductions in usage be accomplished. It is possible to get short-term reductions in usage but without those who work in a facility being involved, the usage invariably crept back up over time. They scheduled meetings with the staff of target areas for reducing consumption. They reviewed monthly bills, showed tracking trends, and then asked employees, "How do we reduce usage?" It is the occupants who then set goals and methods for attainment (Employee Loyalty – Level 4). Facilities staff simply continued to forward monthly tracking sheets and trends to the building team leader.

Here is a short list of what the county has accomplished based on its current efforts.

- Provided employee development for employees and managers.

- Saved 207 Million KWH over a five year period of time.

- Installed automated system controls for air conditioning, lighting, and thermostats, etc.

- Provided limited range thermostats (employees can only move 1-2 degrees).

- Instituted proactive preventative maintenance.

- Replaced T-12 fluorescent bulbs with T-8/T-5 bulbs and induction lights.

- Infrared cameras now used on a membrane roof at sunset to look for water intrusion or improperly connected power lines feeding a motor.

- Required room occupancy sensors on vending machines.

The facilities manager's mantra has become, "Sustainability is not an event, it is a process and a journey. It begins with a small step which can result in big outcomes!" By integrating his people's learning and development, all process improvement, and a strong attitude of environmental consciousness, his department is now helping the Office of Sustainability take the journey and make it count.

The county is a great example of many of our clients that have embraced the six core components of creating a culture of sustainability.

- The organization has a holistic focus on its people, its processes, and the environment, as well as profitability.

- Sustainability is an integral part of the organization's vision and core values.

- There is a top down strategic commitment from senior leadership with employee involvement.

- The organization included its suppliers, constituents, and community in the plan.

- Each aspect of its strategy is specific and measurable with established time commitments.

- The organization has a relentless pursuit of improvement.

What will the next step be for your organization?

Your Next Steps: Getting from Here to There

- CHAPTER NINE -

In the previous chapters, you were introduced to the five levels of business sustainability. No longer is sustainability just about being green. An organization must incorporate sustainable practices in all areas of its operations—people, process, and structure while staying profitable and focusing on what is best for the environment. The original definition of sustainability first coined in 1987 by the Brundtland report still stands: *to meet the needs of the present without compromising the ability of future generations to meet their own needs.* A successful organization meets the current needs for its people, its processes, its customers, and its stakeholders a sustainable organization incorporates strategies that ensure long-term business and environmental sustainability.

So, by reading this book you are obviously headed in the right direction. What steps can and should you take to move forward with your own sustainable initiatives? This chapter captures the questions we posed throughout the book and restates them below, so that you can begin the work of making your organization sustainable. We also offer some activities that will serve to engage your organization's teams in a discussion about what it means to be a sustainable organization. And last, we offer some guidance about when using outside resources to support your sustainability initiatives might make sense for your organization.

As You Get Started – What Questions to Ask? (Chapter One)

1. What definition of sustainability is best for your organization to adopt?

2. What desired results does your organization want to accomplish and in what time frame?

3. How will you measure the desired outcomes?

4. How will you communicate your sustainability plan and establish buy-in with your employees and stakeholders?

5. What is your organization's definition of sustainability?

6. Was your adoption based on regulation, pressure from customers or stakeholders, or internally driven?

7. Who is or should be accountable for sustainability in your organization?

Potential Action Steps

- Conduct the necessary research to better understand what sustainability is and what it could mean to your organization.

- Introduce sustainability as a concept throughout the organization.

- Conduct a senior leadership sustainability awareness workshop.

- Conduct a preliminary or baseline sustainability readiness assessment in order to capture the current state of the organization.

Level One: Recognize and Level Two: Initiate (Chapters Two and Three)

1. If your customers/stakeholders rated your organization on its sustainability initiatives how would the organization fare?

2. Are you currently a 'have to' or an 'it is not necessary' organization?

3. In your organization, what are the top three desired results that could be positively impacted by implementing a strategy of sustainability?

4. What are your customers'/stakeholders' greatest concerns regarding sustainability?

5. How do those concerns relate to your products or services?

6. Is senior leadership committed to a strategy of sustainability?

7. How would your organization benefit if you were to adopt a strategy of sustainability?

8. What is stopping you from implementing a sustainability strategy?

9. If you implemented a strategy of sustainability, how would stakeholder opinion change?

10. What are some quick wins you can implement?

Potential Action Steps

- Conduct a sustainability readiness assessment.

- Conduct senior leadership meetings and/or retreats to open the sustainability discussion and develop roll-out strategies based upon the questions as identified in the getting started section above.

- Identify an outside consultant/coach to facilitate the definition and implementation of sustainability in your organization to maximize results and minimize start-up challenges.

Level Three: Implement (Chapter Four)

1. How are you communicating and engaging your employees in the sustainability initiative?

2. What sustainability measurements are key to your organization?

3. How do you recognize/reward employees who are engaged in the change process?

4. How do you currently use cross-functional teams to tap into the creativity and innovation of those who are closest to your customers and stakeholders?

5. Do you have a process for reporting your sustainability successes?

6. What processes have you realigned in order to support your sustainability efforts?

Potential Action Steps

- Create specific sustainability metrics/measurements across the organization.

- Integrate process improvement and productivity initiatives across the organization.

- Ensure that every team keeps sustainability topics as a standing meeting agenda item.

- Identify an individual to serve as the organization's leader to drive the strategy and manage the implementation plan.

- Create and implement an internal and external communication strategy.

- Conduct a sustainability assessment to measure progress.

Level Four: Operationalize (Chapter Five)

1. What is the long-term sustainability vision for the organization?

2. How is sustainability incorporated into the long-term strategy for the organization?

3. Are current projects aligned with the sustainability vision?

4. How engaged are your employees? How do you know?

5. Are your customers loyal to your products or services? How do you know?

6. How are you measuring your organization's commitment to sustainability?

7. How are you reporting and publicizing your sustainability outcomes?

Potential Action Steps

*   Communicate the long-term organizational sustainability vision to employees, customers, and stakeholders.

*   Ensure that sustainability initiatives are integrated into the organizational strategic plan and annual goals.

*   Discuss sustainability as a part of all hiring processes.

- Conduct a sustainability assessment and measure progress.

Level Five: Transformation

(Chapters Six and Seven)

1. What level of sustainability has your organization obtained? How do you know?

2. What are your next steps?

3. What would it mean for your organization if you were to transform the culture to embed sustainability?

4. Do your customers view your organization as a sustainable one? How do you know?

5. How can a strategy of sustainability differentiate you from your competition?

6. Where are your hidden sustainability opportunities, and how can you capitalize on them today?

7. What process is your organization currently using for giving and receiving sustainability feedback?

8. How can sustainability impact your organization's reputation, customer value, employee retention, and community relations?

Potential Action Steps

- Identify an individual to serve as the organization's leader to drive the strategy and manage the implementation plan. These responsibilities should now be incorporated into this individual's job description, and they should report to the CEO/President.

- Ensure all employee training as well as personal development activities include sustainability components.

- Measure all innovations, customer wins, and internal processes through the lens of sustainability.

- Consistently publish your sustainability goals and accomplishments.

- Serve as a role model for other organizations.

Throughout the book you have had the opportunity to assess where your organization might fall within the levels of integrating sustainability concepts and practices. If at this point you are still not sure where to start, it often helps to begin with some kind of activity that gets your teams thinking creatively. Alex Osborn, who created the term *brainstorming* said it best,

> **"It is easier to tone down a wild idea than to think up a new one."**

Encouraging your staff to be creative and not suppressing wild ideas is crucial to the activities that follow.

These activities can be used within your organization to start a conversation about sustainability, and/or to get a senior leadership team thinking about sustainability issues.

Activity 1: What Do We Value?

If you have existing value statements for your organization, this is a good opportunity to review them and to assess whether or not the statements are still current and appropriate. Giving a team the following set of questions will facilitate a simple activity allowing the team to revisit the corporate values in the context of business sustainability.

- When was the last time we reviewed our organizational values?

- Does our existing value statement still feel relevant?

- How does sustainability fit with those values?

- How might we change our values to incorporate sustainability?

- How would a change in our values statement drive a change in strategic goals?

Once this work is completed, the team needs to consider how to communicate this new set of value statements throughout the organization and how it will include a sustainability message.

Activity 2: Our Sustainable Organization in the Future

Since sustainability initiatives are forward-looking activities, having a vision around where you want to be in the future is crucial. Assuming multiple teams, have each team brainstorm answers to the following question by engaging in one of these optional activities:

Option 1: Ask each team to prepare a short skit illustrating what a sustainable organization looks like in practice. Encourage the teams to use props, humor, and to be creative. Have each team act out its skit.

Option 2: Ask each team to take a blank piece of flip chart paper and draw what a sustainable organization looks like in practice. Encourage the team to use color and interesting illustrations to bring its belief to life. Have each team present its picture to the larger group. Vote on the best illustration and give out prizes to the winning team.

Using an Outside Resource

As you consider the steps you will take in your quest for business sustainability, you may want to engage an outside professional who can help your organization work through the levels of sustainability in a methodical and effective way. An outside facilitator serves as a catalyst, brings new ideas and best practices to the table, and ensures everyone is actively participating in the right activities to drive sustainability. The literal meaning of facilitator is *one who makes things easy.*

Your organization certainly has capable and experienced individuals who can serve as facilitators for this process. However, if internal resources are responsible for the facilitation, then by definition they cannot simultaneously be active participants in the process. If you use a senior leader as the facilitator, then that person's voice does not get heard in the process. An experienced facilitator will foster collaboration, ensure participation, ask good questions, focus on outcomes and results, be mindful of the agenda and timing, capture ideas, and be unbiased. Consider the following thoughts as you determine whether an outside resource would be a helpful part of your sustainability strategy discussions.

- Organizations (and organizational teams) have a strong tendency to define everything in terms of what the organization has done, and will be strongly influenced by the organization's current processes, internal systems, and customs. An outside facilitator will bring a focus beyond current organizational processes.

- If the CEO or COO leads the strategy development, it is virtually assured that the team members will feed him/her what they think he or she wants to hear. An outside facilitator allows everyone to participate and focuses on creating the best plan while not having to worry about the process. An outside facilitator will also be able to challenge the whole thinking process of the group much more effectively as the outside facilitator does not have any agenda other than helping the team develop the best strategy.

- In any new initiative, approximately 10% of the work is in the actual document or records that reflect the strategy. However, 90% of the value of building a sustainability strategy is in the process, the facilitated discussions, the research and data development, the creation of information from the data, the deliberations, and, finally, the process to create conclusions and action steps. To manage that process effectively and efficiently, the facilitator should be outside the internal agenda of the organization. When done well, the process becomes an outstanding team building experience with invaluable and profound outcomes.

- Employee teams can't help but have pre-conceived notions as to where they are going and how to get there. A lot of it will be based on organizational history, some of it internal to the leadership's concept of reality and personal goals. An outside facilitator brings no agenda or history to the process and can draw upon his/her collective experience and expertise when and if appropriate. Effective planning and actions depend on not only an internal assessment and perspective, but also an external one that only comes with the aid of an outside facilitator who can challenge assumptions and information not based in fact.

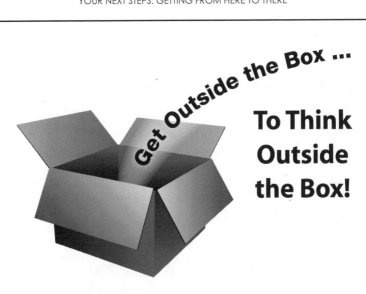

Get Outside the Box ...

To Think Outside the Box!

It has been said that in order to generate out-of-the-box thinking, you must:

- Get outside the box

- Then think

A facilitator who comes from outside your box and asks the right questions significantly increases the chances of generating breakthrough and innovative ideas. Is an outside facilitator the right choice for your organization?

The authors of this book care deeply about making business and environmental sustainability an integral part of our organizations and our work with clients. Through the discussion in these chapters and the information provided, we intend to open your eyes to new approaches for your organization, and to challenge you to consider how incorporating sustainability into your everyday organizational culture is not just the right thing to do, but rather it has become a business imperative. The mega trend of sustainability means your organization must adopt these common sense principles or risk extinction. Organizations that adopt sustainable practices will remain competitive, deliver exceptional market results, and build customer loyalty.

How will you apply these common sense approaches to your sustainability initiatives? When will you start?

About the Authors

Tammy A.S. Kohl

Resource Associates Corporation
www.resourceassociatescorp.com

Tammy A.S. Kohl, President of Resource Associates Corporation (RAC), has been with the corporation since 1986. During that time she has held a series of increasingly responsible positions until her appointment in January 2002 to the current position of President.

Tammy's experience in working with personal clients and a professional network of over 500 RAC Affiliates has given her practical and extensive experience in the areas of creating customer value, understanding business, and generating results. This knowledge and experience is invaluable in establishing the future course of Resource Associates Corporation on a national and international level.

As part of her duties as Executive Vice President she was responsible for managing production, customer service, and Affiliate support areas of the corporation. This knowledge and understanding of running operations and creating efficient processes gives her an in-depth and well rounded working knowledge of how to run a successful business.

In addition to her business sustainability, management, and people skills, she is proficient in setting strategic directions and accomplishing them.

Tammy holds a degree in Business Administration. She is the founder of The Institute for Sustainability.

Betsy Allen

Gaining Results, Inc.
www.GainingResults.com

Betsy Allen has been consulting strategically, training adults, and guiding over 1,000 seminars and performance transformation initiatives for over 20 years. Betsy's clients say that she removes barriers to faster results and sustained competitive advantage. Betsy partners with inspired leaders to clone exceptional qualities, to change what is not working, and to help people reach their potential.

She leverages her Harvard MBA, entrepreneurial and executive experience to advance clients' behavioral change goals. Clients include: Coca-Cola, Edward Lifesciences, Ethicon Endo-Surgery Institute, Glaxo-Smith Kline, Hawaiian Tug & Barge, Johnson & Johnson Diabetes Institute, The Marines, McDonalds, Merck, Microsoft, Oklahoma Human Services, Sony, Vistakon, and Wells Fargo Bank to name a few. Betsy's success as a quality facilitator, business coach, and process improver, allow her to guarantee results and remarkable rewards.

Jim Godshall

Alignment Consultant International
www.ac-llc.com

Jim Godshall is President of Total Quality Institute, Inc., a member of the Institute for Sustainability, and a senior partner of Alignment Consulting International. His consulting experience focuses organizations on aligning their business strategies and processes to achieve quick results and long-term competitive strength. Working with management and employees at all levels in an organization, Jim has facilitated the development and implementation of strategic and business plans, marketing strategies, customer-focused process improvements, cycle time reduction of both business and operating processes, management development from senior management to supervisors, organizational and program assessments, organizational design and Post Merger Integration, and sustainability strategies in such diverse industries as healthcare, hospitality, manufacturing, medical products, distribution, energy, pharmaceutical, government, and service.

Prior to his current career, Jim had over 30 years experience in both professional and consumer product industries at the senior executive level, most recently VP Sales and Marketing at Johnson & Johnson.

He is a graduate of Bucknell University and has completed post graduate work at George Washington University. He is a Certified Quality Facilitator.

Jerry Hogan

The Resource Development Group, LLC
www.resourcedevelopmentgroup.com

After graduating from the United States Naval Academy, Jerry served as a Marine officer for six years. Following his military service, he spent 27 years helping companies grow and prosper through increased sales, decreased expenses, and maximizing an organization's greatest asset—their people. His job functions included virtually all areas: from manufacturing shift foreman to executive vice president of a leading electronic components supplier. Since 2000, Jerry has been the president of The Resource Development Group, LLC, one of the top producing affiliate companies of one of the nation's leading training and development companies.

Jerry brings a wealth of knowledge, experience, and success to his clients. His facilitated development, planning, and sustainability processes have helped organizations in many industries grow and increase profitability. He has worked with clients as small as individual producers and as large as thousands of employees. His clients cover a geographic span from Arizona to Zimbabwe. In addition, Jerry is a sought-after speaker on subjects as diverse as *"The Power of Procrastination"* to *"Sustainability: THE Competitive Advantage."*

Susan Lauer

Aspire Consulting, Ltd.
www.aspireadvantage.com

Susan is co-founder of Aspire Consulting, Ltd., a company committed to helping individuals and organizations that strive to discover personal and professional opportunities and to create measurable improvements. These opportunities always enhance long-term sustainable organizational and individual success. Prior to founding Aspire Consulting in 2006, Susan had a highly successful 25 year career in the healthcare field which strengthened her commitment to life-long professional and personal development. She has held numerous leadership positions with responsibilities that included managing personnel and systems across the health care continuum. She has been a clinical instructor and guest lecturer at the graduate level and has served as an expert in legal proceedings and as a contributing editor for the largest provider of evidence based practice to the insurance industry.

Susan has a Bachelor of Science in Physical Therapy from the University of Connecticut, an Advanced Master's degree with a clinical specialty and healthcare administrative minor as well as a Masters in Public Administration from Long Island University.

Rick Lochner

RPC Leadership Associates, Inc.
www.rpcleadershipassociates.com

Rick Lochner is the President of RPC Leadership Associates, Inc. where he helps business owners, corporate and non-profit leadership teams, and individual professionals make leadership a way of life. Rick is a graduate of the U.S. Military Academy at West Point and spent his 11-year military career leading soldiers in environments ranging from the interior of Alaska to the front lines of Cold War, Europe. After leaving the Army he spent the next 18 years in corporate leadership positions ranging from front-line management to senior executive management. He successfully led organizations in Fortune 100 corporations and privately held entrepreneurial ventures across multiple industries both for-profit and non-profit.

In addition to his undergraduate studies Rick's holds both an MS and MBA. He is a Visiting Professor at the Keller

Graduate School of Management and DeVry University where he teaches a variety of topics including Leadership, Managing Change, and Strategic Management.

Jean Oursler

J. Alden Consulting Group, Inc.
www.jaldenco.com

Jean Oursler is a consultant, speaker, facilitator, and an executive coach who works with clients who are looking to grow. As President of J. Alden Consulting Group, Jean works with Fortune 500 companies, family owned businesses, and closely held organizations in a variety of industries across the globe. She produces tangible results in less than 30 days for her clients ... guaranteed. She is currently working on research on how to develop business elite athletes in American corporations.

Jean has a Masters in organizational development along with several certifications in the following: speaking, coaching, facilitating, career counseling and process improvement. Jean volunteers her time with the Women Presidents Organization, a non-profit whose mission is to help women presidents of multi-million dollar companies grow their businesses to the next level.

Adam Pressman

Success Wright
www.leadershipshape.com

Adam Pressman is a lifelong sailor, captain of a sailing vessel on the East Coast of the United States. Adam leverages the timeless leadership tradition of the intrepid sea captain for businesses and organizations bent on leaving the world a better place than they found it. For three decades Adam has been keeping bad things from happening to good people, first protecting the people, buildings, and information of a diverse spectrum of organizations as large as the Department of Defense to as small as sole proprietorships.

Consistently high resilience and robustness are what Adam establishes for his clients. Such organizations, personnel, and processes better the client results as well as keep them secure and with Adam's experience, his clients achieve more, work less, and celebrate often.

Robyn Rickenbach and Susan Bacher

Springboard International Inc.
www.springboardintl.com

Robyn Rickenbach is the President of Springboard International Inc. She is an innovative, strategic thinker with proven success in executing critical business objectives, making teams successful and facilitating collaboratiye decision making and planning. She has an intense focus on human capital improvement, learning and performance, and organizational development areas with 20 years experience in a variety of market sectors and verticals. Robyn spent almost 15 years in the education sector, as both the Director of Admissions and the President of several career colleges, and in that time also headed self-study teams and implemented new academic programs. She then moved into the corporate world of training and development and helped organizations such as DHL, PricewaterhouseCoopers LLC, and the National Association of College and University Business Officers create and deliver engaging blended learning programs for their audiences. Throughout her career, Robyn's focus has been on developing individuals, teams, and business initiatives to their full potential and executing on critical business goals.

Robyn graduated from the College of William and Mary

with a BA and also holds an MBA from Golden Gate University. She is an active member of the American Society for Training and Development (ASTD) and the D.C. area Women in Technology (WIT) organization. Robyn is also a Certified Business Coach (CBC).

Susan Bacher, a Senior Associate at Springboard International, is a proven business performance professional. Susan has spent the last several years helping clients around the country by analyzing their business processes, facilitating change management, and guiding them through successful technology implementations as a part of Datatel, Inc.

Susan's career has primarily been in the industries of higher education and software implementation, providing both training and consulting to for-profit and non-profit organizations for over 15 years.

Through these experiences she has developed the key skills needed to help individuals and organizations reach their peak performance. Susan holds Bachelor of Arts in Human Services, from Tift College of Mercer University and a Masters of Social Work from the University of Georgia.

Arnold Rintzler

AWR Business Concepts
www.awrintzler.com

Arnold Rintzler is President of AWR Business Concepts in South Orange, New Jersey. Prior to founding AWR Business Concepts in 1993, Arnold spent 29 years in business, including 12 years as President of The Casual Woman, a chain of women's apparel stores which he founded, grew successfully, and sold to a national apparel retailer. His senior management responsibilities also include eight years with the R.H. Macy Company and six years with Federated Department Stores, where his diverse experiences encompassed all aspects of buying, store merchandising, operations, and human resources, as well as new store planning and construction, and renovations of existing stores.

Arnold has also worked directly as a consultant and Executive Coach to principals in a wide variety of industries including manufacturing, construction, retailing, professional, and service industries. He has worked with organizations, both public and private, on management issues, process improvement, and strategic direction. Arnold assists organizations and businesses to implement a holistic business approach to continuous process improvement (TQM). Working with management and staff at all levels of an organization, he has facilitated the development of strategic and business plans, marketing strategies, leadership, management, sales development skills and employee evaluations. Arnold has a Degree in Psychology from the University of Pittsburgh.

Greg Stuart

Harmony Solutions International, LLC
www.harmonypps.com

Greg Stuart is a Certified Business Coach (CBC) with Harmony Solutions International, LLC, a woman-owned business in Westlake Village, California and an Adjunct Professor of Leadership and Ethics in Masters in Public Policy and Administration (MPPA) at California Lutheran University. Greg is passionate about the environment and believes that connecting with people is key for leadership development. At 27, he became the youngest-ever President of the Los Angeles Junior Chamber of Commerce–the second largest in the world. Today, Greg sponsors an ongoing Leadership Summit series designed to engage community leaders in issues of concern.

Greg converted his vehicle to run on vegetable oil in 2005. He competes in adventure races and other extreme sports including becoming an age-group national champion in an

8-mile ocean swim. He has competed in over 30 marathons, including Boston, and supported a participant in finishing the 135 mile Badwater foot race through Death Valley in 135 degree heat in July.

With his wife, Elaine, and their three children, Greg completed a one-year RV journey throughout North America in 2004, visiting 3 countries, 49 National Park Service units, and 40 states.

Grant Tate

the bridge, ltd
www.thebridge-ltd.com

Grant Tate is the cofounder and CEO of the bridge, ltd of Charlottesville, VA. Mix in equal parts of corporate experience, entrepreneurial zeal, public service, business advocacy, teaching, and a passion for excellence and you get Grant Tate. Grant is famous for saying:

"Experience is our competitive edge. We have the MBAs and we know the theories, but we've found over the years of doing this, that there is no substitute for real-world experience. We've been there, done that. We know what works, and we know how to communicate that knowledge. But we have also learned that no amount of knowledge works, unless there is also a genuine concern for the growth and success of others."

In 1992, he took the company to Europe, founded a Dutch BV, and spent five years researching technology trends for the European Commission. He is the founder of three small companies and was co-founder of the New Mexico Technical Innovation Center and the Connecticut Venture Center–organizations formed to help formulate and grow entrepreneurial companies. Before starting the bridge, ltd, Grant was an executive at IBM where he led a software development lab, introduced new products, and managed reorganization of a $2 billion hi-tech division.

Models

Model 1.1

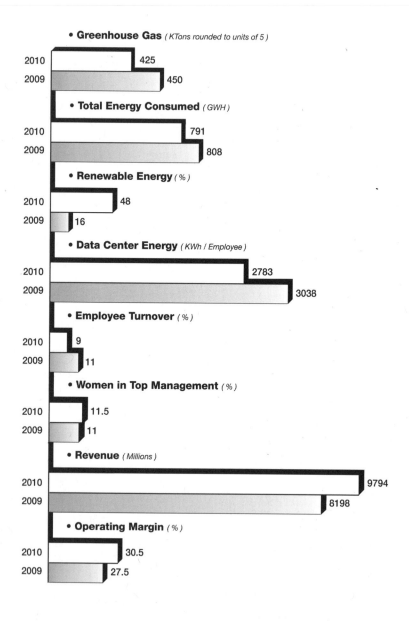

• Greenhouse Gas *(KTons rounded to units of 5)*

2010 425
2009 450

• Total Energy Consumed *(GWH)*

2010 791
2009 808

• Renewable Energy *(%)*

2010 48
2009 16

• Data Center Energy *(KWh / Employee)*

2010 2783
2009 3038

• Employee Turnover *(%)*

2010 9
2009 11

• Women in Top Management *(%)*

2010 11.5
2009 11

• Revenue *(Millions)*

2010 9794
2009 8198

• Operating Margin *(%)*

2010 30.5
2009 27.5

Model 2.1

| | 10 | 20 | 30 | 40 | 50 | 60 | 70 | 80 | 90 | 100 |

Reducing costs through improved materials efficiency.

1 — 72%

Manufacturing or sourcing domestically/locally.

2 — 58%

Increasing brand awareness as green or socially responsible.

3 — 53%

Designing and offering sustainable products/services.

4 — 52%

Providing customers with more information about products'/ services' social and environmental impacts.

5 — 50%

Offering more energy efficient products/services.

6 — 48%

Providing frontline employees with business training to broaden and improve commercial awareness.

7 — 46%

Using sustainability as a market differentiator.

8 — 22%

Model 2.2
A Common Sense Approach to Sustainability

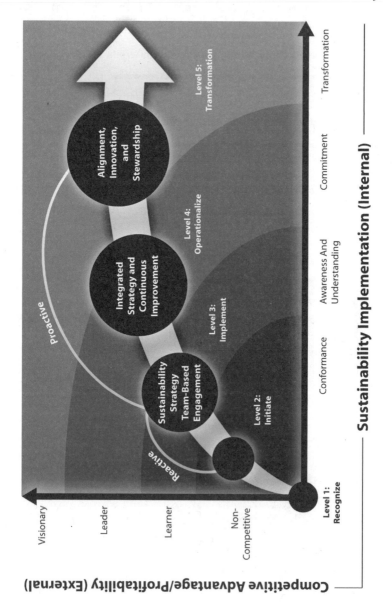

Model 4.1

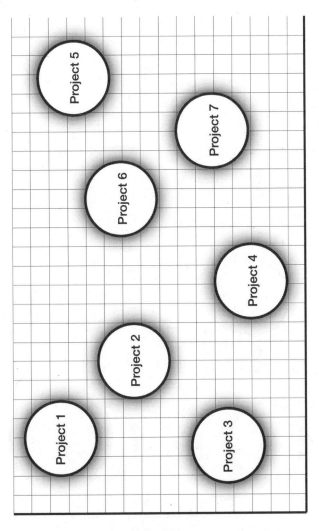

Project Value Chart

Model 4.2

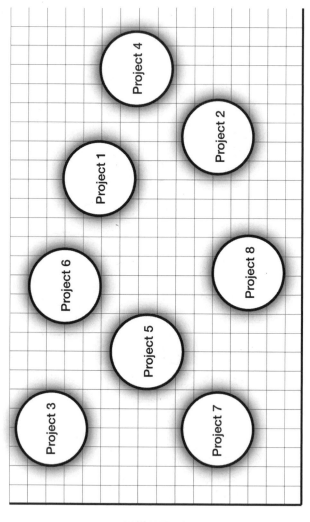

Project Value Chart

Time to Implement

Benefit

Project 4
Project 2
Project 1
Project 6
Project 8
Project 5
Project 3
Project 7

Model 4.3

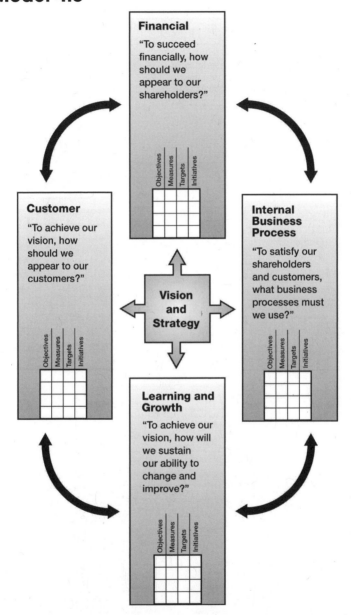

Model 4.4

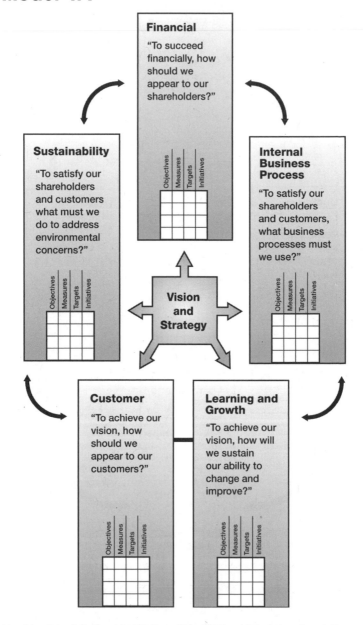

Adapted from Robert S. Kaplan and David P. Norton, "Using the Balanced Score Card as a Strategic Management System," Harvard Business Review (January-February 1996): 76.

Model 8.1

Sustainability Implementation Model

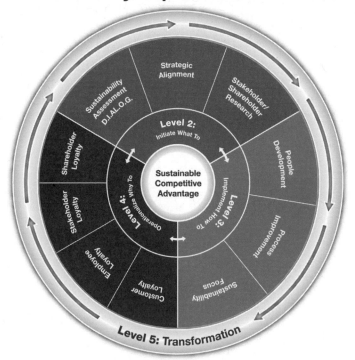

Level 2: Initiate What To
Sustainability Assessment D.I.AL.O.G.
Strategic Alignment
Shareholder/Stakeholder Research

Level 3: Implement How To
People Development
Process Improvement
Sustainability Focus

Level 4: Operationalize Why To
Customer Loyalty
Employee Loyalty
Stakeholder Loyalty
Shareholder Loyalty

Level 5: Transformation

Resources

BBMG. Unleashed: How New Consumers Will Revolutionize Brands and Scale Sustainability (March 2011) http://bbmg.com/how/new-consumer-download/ Chapter 5, Page 51

Berea College. Case Study. http://www. berea.edu/sens/ Chapter 1, Page 6

Boston College. Study. The State of Corporate Citizenship in the United States 2009, http://www. bcccc.net/index.cfm?fuseaction=document.showDocu mentByID&DocumentID=1333 Chapter 2, Page 12

Boston Consulting Group. Report. The Business of Sustainability, 2009. www.bcg.com/ documents/file29480.pdf Chapter 1, Page 2

Canadian Tire Company. Case Study. http://
corp.canadiantire.ca/EN/MAD/Pages/
default.aspx Chapter 7, Page 65

Ceres Conference. 2011 Award Winners. http://www.
ceres.org/awards/reporting-awards Chapter 3, Page 25

Collins and Porras. Built to Last: Successful
Habits of Visionary Companies. Harper Business
Essentials. (2002) Chapter 5, Page 47

Dell. 2011 Corporate Sustainability Report. http://content.
dell.com/us/en/corp/report.aspx Chapter 2, Page 19

Hitchcock and Willard. The Business Guide to
Sustainability: Practical Strategies and Tools for
Organizations. Routledge (2009) Chapter 7, page 60

Johnson Financial Group. Case Study. http://www.
americanbanker.com/btn/23_4/mid-tier-banks-
johnson-financial-saves-green-by-going-green-
1016580-1.html Introduction, Page XI

Patagonia. The Footprint Chronicles. http://www.
patagonia.com/us/footprint/index.jsp Chapter 1, Page 3

SAP. Report. http://www.sapsustainabilityreport.
com/operations-impact, Chapter 1, Page 4

Small Business Administration. www.sba.gov/
advocacy/7495/8420 Introduction, Page XIII

Standing Stone Brewing Company. Case
Study. http://www.standingstonebrewing.
com/sustainability.html Chapter 5, Page 44

United Nations World Commission on Environment and Development. Brundtland Report. http://www.un-documents.net/wced-ocf.htm Chapter 1, Page 1

Walmart. 2009 Sustainability Report. http://walmartstores.com/Sustainability/ Introduction, Page IX